A Kids Coloring & Funny Joke Book

Discover the Pacific Northwest

by RuthAnn Cole

This book belongs to:

_____

HAHAHA & Hmm...

Ready for a PNW adventure without leaving your seat?

This travel guide in book form has it all—coloring pages from easy to difficult to "Whoa, this is tricky!", riddles that'll make you think, and jokes so funny you'll snort.

You'll explore West Coast attractions, meet some quirky animals (on paper, thankfully), and dive into all the fun the Pacific Northwest has to offer. So grab your crayons and sense of humor—it's time to explore and color your way through the Pacific Northwest!

Black Bears

Why don't bears wear shoes?

Because they have bear feet!

Potato Farms in Idaho

What do you get if you cross an elephant with a Potato?

Mashed Potatoes!

Prehistoric Gardens in Oregon

What do you get when a dinosaur crashes its car?

Tyrannosaurus Wrecks!

Sand Dunes in Oregon

What did the sand dune say to the ATV rider?

"Wheelie" good job getting up here!

PNW Fruit Trees

What's a tree's favorite drink?

"Root" beer!

Soda Springs Geyser in Idaho

What did the geyser feel when it was complimented?

It was erupting with joy!

PNW Ferry Boats

Why did the ferry feel nervous?

It was sailing in uncharted waters!

"Count the spud-tacular ways to use a potato!"

Why did the potato salad blush?

Because it saw the salad dressing!

Washington Riddles

1
I soar above the city, tall and proud,
On a clear day, I draw a curious crowd.
A needle with a sweeping view,
Who am I? Can you guess too?

2
I'm a mountain with snow on top,
But I'm not just for skiing—I can pop!
When I blew my top, ash filled the air,
Which Washington volcano gave everyone a scare?

3
I'm not a canyon, but I'm super wide,
With cliffs and a river flowing by my side.
Concerts here are epic and loud,
What's my name? I draw quite a crowd!

4
You can't drive across where I take you,
Just ride and enjoy the water view.
To the islands and back—it's a busy scene,
What am I, the state's water queen?

5
I wake you up with a cup in hand,
I'm the most famous brew across the land.
I started in Seattle, where coffee is king,
What's my name? I'm a caffeine thing!

6
In a rainforest that's super green,
The tallest trees you've ever seen.
There's moss and fog—kind of spooky too,
But the beauty here will amaze you!

7
I'm a city where rivers roar and parks are grand,
You can ride a gondola right over the land.
With a giant red wagon that's tons of fun,
What Washington city is this lively one?

ANSWERS
1 - The Space Needle
2 - Mount St. Helens
3 - The Gorge Amphitheater
4 - Washington Ferries
5 - Starbucks Coffee
6 - Olympic National Park
7 - Spokane

Oregon Riddles

1

I twist and turn and rush to the sea,
Dividing two states, who could I be?
From snowy peaks to ocean's roar,
I bring life and power to the Pacific
Northwest shore.

2

I was a path for those seeking new life,
Full of adventure, hardship, and strife.
What trail am I that made history's mark,
Leading the way like Lewis and Clark?

3

I'm a giant blue bowl, deep and wide,
With a mountain for an island inside.
People come from far and near
To see my waters, crystal clear.

4

I'm creamy, I'm tasty, I'm found in a store,
You'll spot me along the Oregon coast shore.
Some say I'm sharp, some say I'm mild,
I make grilled cheese dreams for every child!

5

I'm a city where bridges soar,
With doughnuts, books, and coffee galore.
You can "Keep it Weird" and bike downtown—
What Oregon city wears this crown?

6

I stand tall in Cannon Beach's sand,
A rock with views that look quite grand.
At low tide, I wear tidepools at my feet—
What famous rock might you meet?

7

I'm not in a pond, though I quack with pride,
At sporting events, I'm on Oregon's side.
With green and yellow, I charge down the track—
What famous team never holds back?

ANSWERS

1 – The Columbia River
2 – The Oregon Trail
3 – Crater Lake
4 – Tillamook Cheese
5 – Portland
6 – Haystack Rock
7 – The Oregon Ducks

Idaho Riddles

1
I'm buried in dirt till I'm ready to eat.
I'm mashed or fried—there's no way I'm beat!
You can stack me in chips or make me a fry.
What veggie am I? Come on, give it a try!

2
I carve through valleys, I twist and I roar.
My waters rush fast, from mountains I pour.
Grab a raft or a boat if you're feeling brave.
Which famous river makes a big wave?

3
People search for me near rivers and lakes.
A shiny red gemstone from Idaho it takes.
Found deep in the earth, I'm a colorful prize.
What gem do treasure hunters idolize?

4
My summit is snowy, my height is supreme.
I'm the tallest in Idaho—a climber's dream.
Far above valleys, I rise to the sky.
What mountain is this that's standing so high?

5
I'm small and I'm fast with feathers of blue.
In Idaho skies, I soar past you.
I'm the state bird, if you need a clue.
What kind of bird am I? Bet you knew!

6
I'm a valley of rocks in shapes so bizarre,
Like giants or castles—some near, some far.
Come hike through my trails and explore each bend.
What Idaho wonder am I, my friend?

7
I bubble and steam, I'm relaxing and hot.
People love soaking in this scenic spot.
With mountains around and no need for a tub.
Where in Idaho do you find a hot hub?

ANSWERS
1 - The Potato
2 - The Snake River
3 - Garnet
4 - Mount Borah
5 - Mountain Bluebird
6 - City of Rocks
7 - Hot Springs

White Tailed Deer

Why did the deer need braces?

Because it had "buck" teeth!

Mt. Bachelor in Oregon

What do you call a funny mountain?

Hill-arious!

Silverwood Theme Park in Idaho

What's a ferris wheel's life motto?

"What goes around comes around!"

PNW Sea Otter

Why did the sea otter sit on the rock?

Because it wanted to be a rock star!

Salmon

What's a salmon's favorite instrument?

The bass guitar!

Idaho Jokes

Q: Why didn't the astronaut need to visit Craters of the Moon?
A: Because Idaho's version was already out of this world!

Q: Why did the hiker bring a pen to the top of the Sawtooth Mountains?
A: To draw breath-taking views!

Q: Why did the huckleberry never get into trouble?
A: Because it was always berry well-behaved!

Q: Why did the roller coaster at Silverwood refuse to slow down?
A: It wanted to stay on track!

Q: What's a computer's favorite snack in Idaho?
A: Micro-chips!

Q: Why do Idaho farmers never share their secrets?
A: Because they want to keep things rooted in tradition!

Q: Why did the Idaho fish refuse to play hide-and-seek?
A: Because it always got caught!

Q: Why did the gemstone go to Idaho?
A: To find its true sparkle!

Q: What did one fish say to the other in the Snake River?
A: "Water we waiting for? Let's make some waves!"

Q: Why don't bears in Idaho use cell phones?
A: Because they can't bear the roaming charges!

Oregon Jokes

Q: Why did the Oregonian bring a berry to the party?
A: Because it was ready to Jam!

Q: Why did the beaver build a dam in Oregon?
A: Because it Otter make it its home!

Q: Why did the tree move to Oregon?
A: It wanted to branch out in the forest!

Q: Why did the crab refuse to share its treasure at Cannon Beach?
A: Because it was being a little shellfish!

Q: What's Crater Lake's favorite type of party?
A: A Pool Party!

Q: Why did the Ferris wheel get kicked out of Oaks Park?
A: It kept going in circles during conversations!

Q: Why are Portland bridges so good at friendships?
A: They're great at connecting people!

Q: What do you call a bear who gets lost at Silver Falls?
A: A drizzly bear!

Q: Why do windsurfers love the Columbia River Gorge?
A: Because they're blown away every time!

Q: What do you call a seagull that lives near the bay instead of the ocean?
A: A bagel!

Washington Jokes

Q: Why is Washington so good at hide and seek?
A: Because it's always covered in mist!

Q: What's a barista's favorite workout in Seattle?
A: The espresso press!

Q: What did the octopus say when it swam off the coast of Washington?
A: "This place is ink-credible!"

Q: Why did the cloud refuse to leave Washington State?
A: It felt right at home!

Q: What did the Space Needle say to the Monorail?
A: "I'm always here to give you a lift!"

Q: Why did the whale go to the San Juan Islands?
A: To take a kriller vacation!

Q: What's the North Cascades' favorite kind of movie?
A: Cliff-hangers!

Q: Why don't people ever tell Mount Rainier secrets?
A: Because it might erupt with excitement!

Q: What's the noisiest thing at Pike Place Market?
A: The fish—they're always flipping out!

Q: What's Washington's state song for lazy days?
A: "Raindrops Keep Falling on My Head"!

WASHINGTON

Elk

Why did the elk join the school band?

Because it heard they needed a good horn player!

Looff Carousel in Washington

What do you call a horse on a carousel that can't stop dancing?

A whirl and twirl!

Dragonfly

What do dragonflies use to keep in touch with their friends?

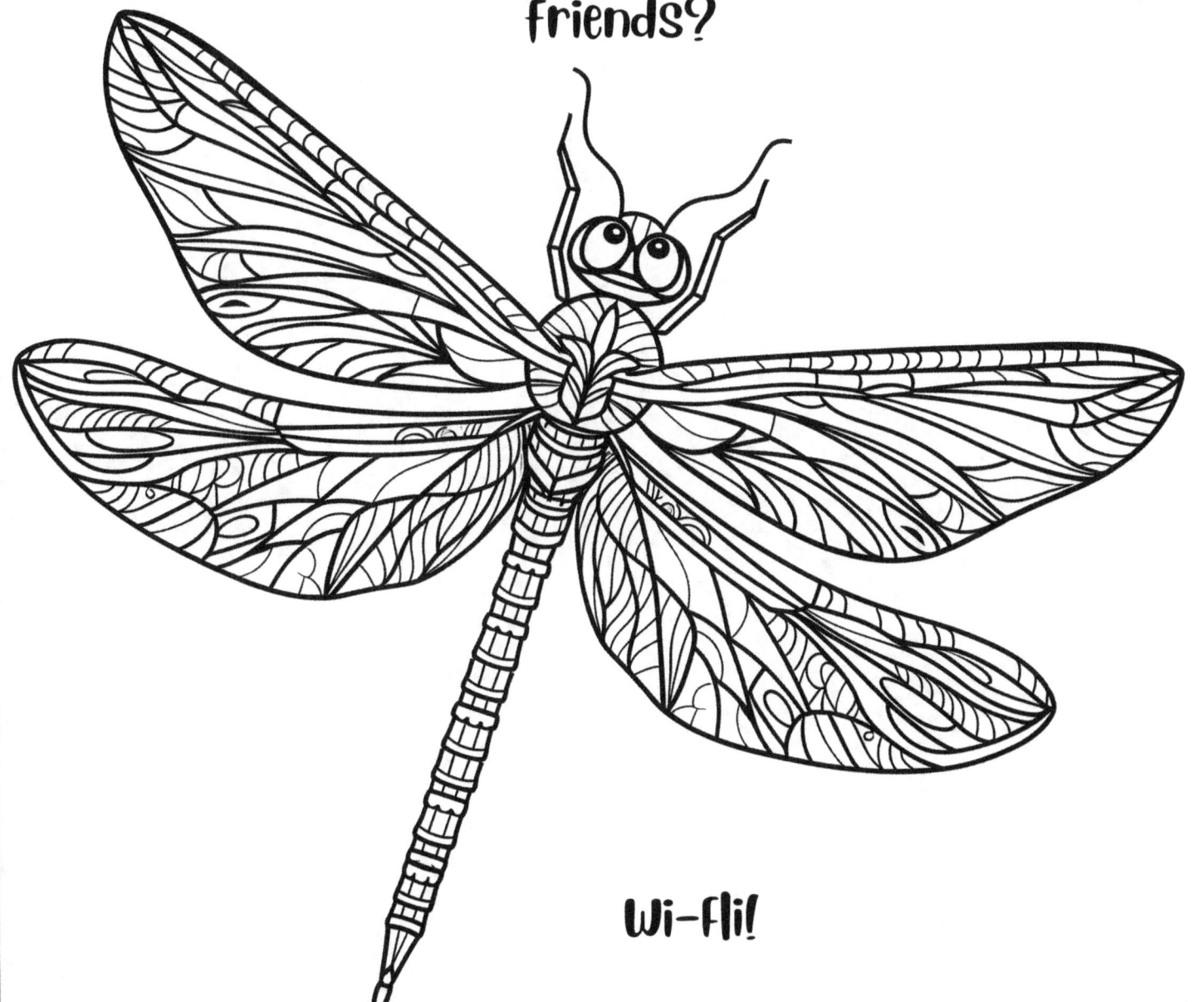

Wi-fli!

Oregon

What is an Oregonian's favorite type of math?

Tree-ometry!

Idaho

Why did the Potato go to the Party in Idaho?

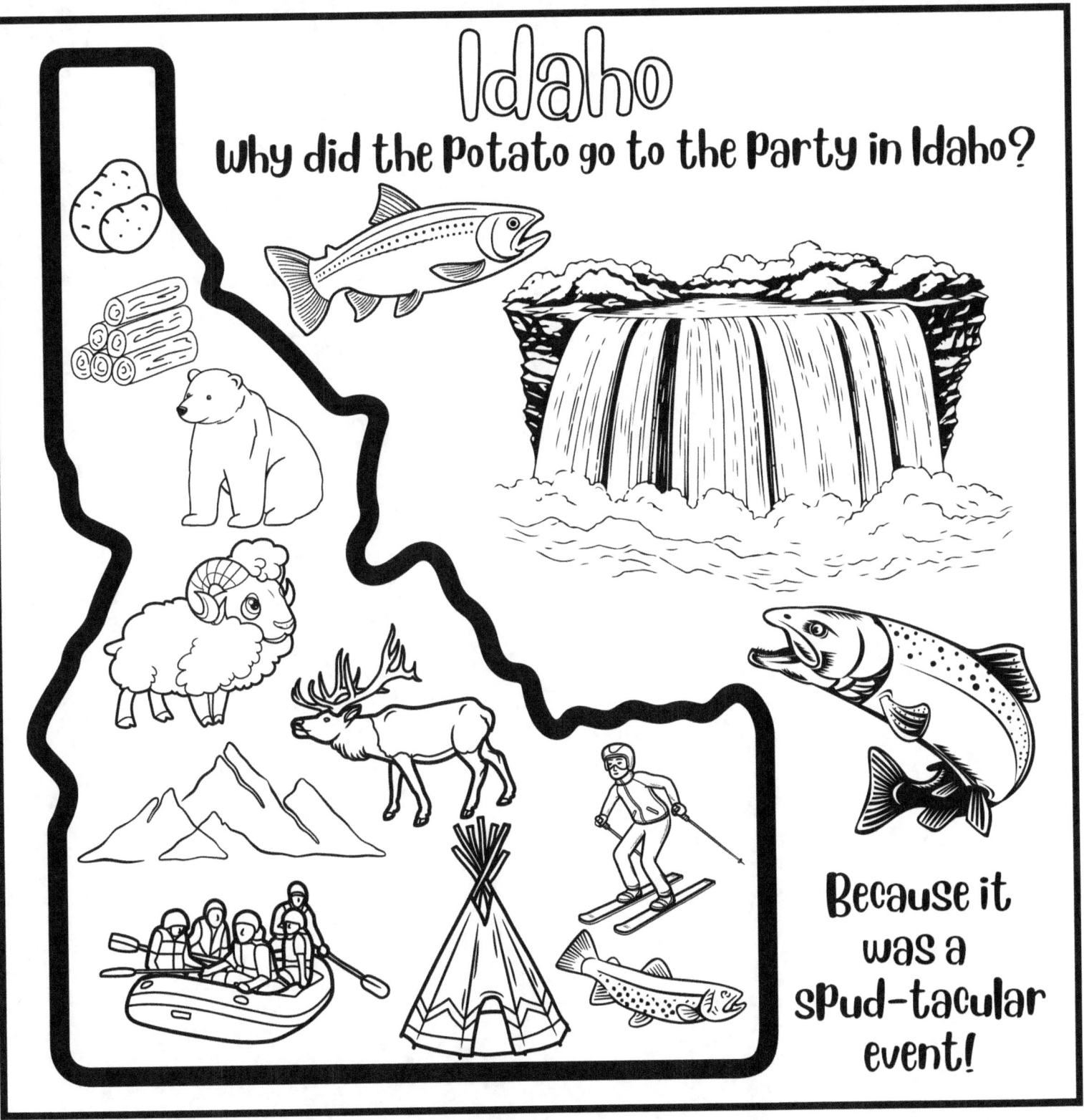

Because it was a spud-tacular event!

Washington

What is Washington's favorite kind of music?

Rain 'n' Roll!

Other Pacific Northwest books by this author include:

Little Prayers for Big Feelings

A Children's Book on Emotions

Pacific Northwest Travel Guide – Quirky & Unusual Places to Visit

Pacific Northwest Travel Guide & Stories

About the Author

RuthAnn is a retired teacher who loves making learning as fun as possible! She's an M&M's and travel fanatic, lives with her family in Washington state, and is on the lookout for the next unexpected twist in life!

"Educational, hilarious, and perfect for road trip coloring!"
- A Pacific Northwest Mom

"I love how you used Pacific Northwest wildlife to help kids discover what's right in their own backyard. Let's go explore!"
- Jerry P.

Reviews Wanted!

Make someone laugh! Share why this book works for your kids and children, and maybe include your favorite joke too!

https://a.co/d/2jFuyFy

www.ingramcontent.com/pod-product-compliance
Lightning Source LLC
Chambersburg PA
CBHW080846120626
46553CB00009B/2595